main
soups

The Family Circle® Promise of Success

Welcome to the world of Confident Cooking, created for you in the
Family Circle® Test Kitchen, where recipes are double-tested by our team
of home economists to achieve a high standard of success.

MURDOCH
B O O K S

MAKING STOCK

Homemade stocks make a rich, full-flavoured base for a variety of soups. Take the time to make your own and store in the refrigerator or freezer until ready to use—your family's tastebuds will appreciate it.

BEEF STOCK
Preheat the oven to hot 220°C (425°F/Gas 7). Trim 2 kg beef bones of fat and sinew. Place the bones in a greased roasting tin and roast for 40 minutes. Add 2 chopped leeks, 2 chopped carrots and 2 chopped celery sticks. Roast for 35 minutes, tossing the vegetables occasionally. Transfer the bones and vegetables to a large saucepan or stockpot. Remove any excess fat from the tin without discarding the meat juices. Add 1 cup (250 ml) cold water to the tin, scraping up any sediment stuck to the bottom. Transfer the liquid to the saucepan. Add 1 chopped leek, 1 bouquet garni (see Note), 6 peppercorns and 5 litres cold water. Bring to the boil over high heat, skimming any scum that rises to the surface. Reduce the heat and simmer gently for 4 hours, skimming

as necessary and adding more water if needed (the water should always just cover the ingredients). Strain the stock through a fine sieve into a heatproof bowl. Do not press on the solids or it may cloud the stock. Cover and refrigerate overnight. Remove the layer of fat on the surface. Will keep refrigerated for 3–4 days, or frozen for up to 4 months. Makes about 2 litres.

CHICKEN STOCK
Place 2 kg chicken bones, 1 chopped onion, 1 chopped carrot, 1 chopped celery stick, 1 chopped leek, 1 bay leaf, a few stalks of parsley, 1 sprig thyme, 8 peppercorns and 6 litres cold water in a large saucepan or stockpot. Bring to the boil over high heat, skimming any scum that rises to the surface. Reduce the heat and simmer for 2–3 hours, continuing to skim as

needed. Strain the stock through a fine sieve into a heatproof bowl. Do not press on the solids or it may cloud the stock. Cover and refrigerate overnight. Remove the layer of fat. Will keep refrigerated for 3–4 days, or frozen for up to 4 months. Makes about 3.5 litres.

ROAST VEGETABLE STOCK
Preheat the oven to moderately hot 200°C (400°F/Gas 6). Combine 1 large quartered onion, 3 carrots cut into large pieces, 6 smashed garlic cloves, 1 turnip cut into large pieces, 1 swede cut into large pieces, 1 sliced fennel bulb, 250 g Swiss brown mushrooms and 1 tablespoon oil in a roasting tin, then roast for 1 hour. Transfer to a large saucepan or stockpot. Add 1 cup (250 ml) cold water to the tin, scraping up any sediment stuck to the bottom, then transfer to the pan. Add 1 bouquet garni (see Note), 6 peppercorns and 1.75 litres cold water. Season. Slowly bring to a simmer over low heat for 1 hour. Strain the stock through a fine sieve into a heatproof bowl, pressing the vegetables to extract the juices. Season. Will keep refrigerated for 2–3 days, or frozen for up to 4 months. Makes about 1.25 litres.

FISH STOCK
Place 2 kg white fish bones and trimmings (remove any eyes with a teaspoon) in a bowl of salted water. Stand for 10 minutes, then drain. Transfer to a large saucepan or stockpot with 1 chopped onion, 1 chopped celery stick, 1 bay leaf, 6 peppercorns, the juice of 1 lemon and 2 litres cold water. Bring to the boil, skimming any scum that rises to the surface. Reduce the heat and simmer for 20 minutes, continuing to skim as needed. Strain through a fine sieve into a heatproof bowl. Do not press on the solids or it may cloud the stock. Will keep refrigerated for 2–3 days, or frozen for up to 3 months. Makes 1.5 litres.

Note: A bouquet garni is a bundle of herbs tied together with string. It usually consists of thyme, parsley, celery leaves and bay leaves.

HEARTY SOUPS

TOMATO SOUP WITH GRILLED MOZZARELLA AND BASIL SANDWICHES

Prep time: 25 minutes
Cooking time: 2 hours
Serves 4–6

1.5 kg Roma tomatoes, halved lengthways
2 teaspoons chopped fresh thyme leaves
1 teaspoon sea salt
21/2 tablespoons olive oil
2 onions, chopped
4 large cloves garlic, crushed
1/4 teaspoon chilli flakes
400 g can tomatoes
1.5 litres chicken stock
1 cup (15 g) fresh basil, torn
1 tablespoon balsamic vinegar

Grilled sandwiches
1 loaf crusty Italian bread, cut into twelve 1 cm slices
21/2 tablespoons extra virgin olive oil
1 clove garlic, cut in half
1 cup (15 g) fresh basil, torn
320 g mozzarella, sliced

1 Preheat the oven to moderately hot 200°C (400°F/Gas 6). Place the tomatoes (cut-side-up) on a large, lined baking tray. Sprinkle with the thyme and salt, drizzle with 11/2 tablespoons of the oil, then roast for 1 hour.
2 Heat the remaining oil in a saucepan over medium heat. Cook the onion, stirring, for 10 minutes, or until soft and starting to brown. Add the garlic and cook for 30 seconds. Add the roast tomatoes and any juices, the chilli flakes, canned tomatoes, stock and basil. Bring to the boil, reduce the heat and simmer, covered, for 40 minutes.
3 Blend the soup until smooth and return to the cleaned pan. Stir in the vinegar (with a pinch of sugar, if necessary).

GRILLED SANDWICHES
1 Heat a chargrill plate over high heat. Brush each side of the bread slices using 11/2 tablespoons of the oil, then chargrill for 3–4 minutes on each side, or until golden. Rub the garlic onto one side of each slice.
2 Place six slices of bread on a baking tray (garlic-side-up), then top with the basil and mozzarella. Drizzle with the leftover oil. Grill for 1 minute to melt the cheese. Top with the remaining slices of bread and cut in half. Serve with the hot soup.

Nutrition per serve (6): Fat 27 g; Protein 25 g; Carbohydrate 34 g; Dietary Fibre 6.5 g; Cholesterol 33.5 mg; 1990 kJ (475 Cal)

RAVIOLI BROTH WITH LEMON AND BABY SPINACH

Prep time: 15 minutes + overnight refrigeration
Cooking time: 3 hours 35 minutes
Serves 4

Stock
1.5 kg chicken bones (necks, backs, wings)
2 large leeks, chopped
2 large carrots, chopped
2 large celery sticks, chopped
6 sprigs fresh lemon thyme
4 fresh flat-leaf parsley stalks
10 black peppercorns

360 g fresh veal ravioli
2 strips lemon rind (6 cm long), white pith removed
150 g baby English spinach leaves, stems removed
1/2 teaspoon lemon oil
1–2 tablespoons lemon juice
1/2 cup (40 g) shaved Parmesan

1 Place the chicken bones in a large saucepan with 3 litres cold water. Bring to a simmer over medium–low heat (do not boil) for 30 minutes, removing any scum that rises to the surface. Add the remaining stock ingredients and simmer, partially covered, for 3 hours. Strain through a fine sieve and cool. Cover and refrigerate overnight. Remove the layer of fat on the surface.
2 Place the stock in a large saucepan and bring to the boil. Add the ravioli and rind, and cook for 3–5 minutes, or until the ravioli floats to the top and is tender. Stir in the spinach and season. Discard the rind, and just before serving, stir in the lemon oil (to taste) and lemon juice. Garnish with Parmesan.

Nutrition per serve: Fat 11.5 g; Protein 20 g; Carbohydrate 36 g; Dietary Fibre 4 g; Cholesterol 32.5 mg; 1360 kJ (325 Cal)

CREAMY CHICKEN AND CORN SOUP

Prep time: 15 minutes
Cooking time: 1 hour 20 minutes
Serves 4–6

20 g butter
1 tablespoon olive oil
500 g chicken thigh fillets, trimmed and thinly sliced
2 cloves garlic, chopped
1 leek, chopped
1 large celery stick, chopped
1 bay leaf
1/2 teaspoon fresh thyme
1 litre chicken stock
1/4 cup (60 ml) sherry
4 cups (550 g) corn kernels (fresh, canned or frozen)
1 large floury potato (russet), cut into 1 cm cubes
3/4 cup (185 ml) cream, plus extra to drizzle
fresh chives, to garnish

1 Melt the butter and oil in a large saucepan over high heat. Cook the chicken in batches for 3 minutes, or until lightly golden and just cooked through. Place in a bowl, cover and refrigerate until needed.
2 Reduce the heat to medium, and stir in the garlic, leek, celery, bay leaf and thyme for 2 minutes, or until the leek softens—do not allow the garlic to burn. Add the stock, sherry and 2 cups (500 ml) water and stir, scraping up any sediment stuck to the bottom of the pan. Add the corn and potato and bring to the boil. Reduce the heat and simmer for 1 hour, skimming any scum off the surface. Cool slightly.
3 Remove the bay leaf and purée the soup. Return to the cleaned pan, add the cream and chicken and stir over medium–low heat for 2–3 minutes, or until heated through—do not boil. Season. Drizzle with extra cream and garnish with chives. Serve with crusty bread.

Nutrition per serve (6): Fat 26.5 g; Protein 23 g; Carbohydrate 22 g; Dietary Fibre 5.5 g; Cholesterol 123.5 mg; 1780 kJ (425 Cal)

Ravioli broth with lemon and baby spinach (top), and Creamy chicken and corn soup

PUMPKIN SOUP WITH SAGE PESTO

Prep time: 20 minutes
Cooking time: 40 minutes
Serves 4

1 kg butternut pumpkin, peeled, seeded and chopped
2 floury potatoes (russet), chopped
2 large onions, chopped
1.5 litres chicken stock
pinch ground nutmeg
1/2 cup (125 ml) cream

Sage pesto
1/2 cup (8 g) fresh sage
11/4 cups (20 g) fresh flat-leaf parsley
2 cloves garlic, crushed
1 tablespoon pine nuts, toasted
1/3 cup (30 g) walnuts, toasted
2 tablespoons olive oil
2 tablespoons extra virgin olive oil
1/2 teaspoon sea salt
1/4 cup (25 g) freshly grated Parmesan

1 Place the pumpkin, potato, onion and stock in a large saucepan and bring to the boil over high heat. Reduce the heat and simmer for 25–30 minutes, or until the vegetables are soft.
2 To make the sage pesto, process the sage, parsley, garlic, pine nuts, walnuts, olive oils and sea salt in a food processor until smooth. Transfer to a small bowl and stir in the Parmesan. Season to taste.
3 Cool the soup slightly and blend in batches in a blender until smooth. Return to the cleaned saucepan and season with nutmeg, salt and pepper. Stir in the cream and reheat over medium heat until warmed through. Serve, topped with a little sage pesto.

Nutrition per serve: Fat 43.5 g; Protein 17 g; Carbohydrate 35 g; Dietary Fibre 7 g; Cholesterol 48 mg; 2475 kJ (590 Cal)

OXTAIL SOUP WITH STOUT AND VEGETABLES

Prep time: 2 hours
Cooking time: 4 hours 15 minutes
Serves 4

2 kg oxtails, trimmed
2 tablespoons vegetable oil
2 onions, finely chopped
1 leek, finely chopped
2 carrots, diced
1 celery stick, diced
2 cloves garlic, crushed
2 bay leaves
2 tablespoons tomato paste
1 sprig fresh thyme
2 fresh flat-leaf parsley stalks
3.5 litres chicken stock
11/2 cups (375 ml) stout
2 tomatoes, seeded and diced
100 g cauliflower florets
100 g green beans
100 g broccoli florets
100 g asparagus, cut into 3 cm lengths

1 Preheat the oven to moderately hot 200°C (400°F/Gas 6). Place the oxtails in a baking dish and bake for 1 hour, turning occasionally, or until dark golden. Cool.
2 Heat the oil in a large saucepan over medium heat and cook the onion, leek, carrot and celery for 3–4 minutes, or until soft. Stir in the garlic, bay leaves and tomato paste, then add the oxtails, thyme and parsley stalks. Add the stock and bring to the boil over high heat. Reduce the heat and simmer for 3 hours, or until the oxtails are tender and the meat falls off the bone. Skim off any scum that rises to the surface. Remove the oxtails and cool slightly.
3 Take the meat off the bones, discarding any fat or sinew. Roughly chop and add to the soup with the stout, tomato and 2 cups (500 ml) water. Add the vegetables and simmer for 5 minutes, or until tender. Season.

Nutrition per serve: Fat 21.5 g; Protein 47 g; Carbohydrate 20 g; Dietary Fibre 7 g; Cholesterol 88.5 mg; 2065 kJ (495 Cal)

Pumpkin soup with sage pesto (top), and Oxtail soup with stout and vegetables

LENTIL SOUP WITH GRILLED PROSCIUTTO AND ROCKET SALAD

Prep time: 25 minutes +
  10 minutes standing
Cooking time:
  1 hour 45 minutes
Serves 4

1 ham bone (400 g)
11/2 cups (280 g) green or
  brown lentils
2 tablespoons olive oil
80 g butter
2 onions, finely chopped
3 cloves garlic, crushed
1 carrot, diced
1 celery stick, diced
400 g can diced tomatoes
1.5 litres chicken stock
1 bay leaf
2 tablespoons finely
  chopped fresh flat-leaf
  parsley
1/4 cup (25 g) finely grated
  Parmesan

*Prosciutto and rocket
  salad*
80 g thinly sliced prosciutto
140 g rocket leaves
1/2 small red onion,
  finely chopped
1 tablespoon lemon juice
2 tablespoons olive oil
1/4 cup (25 g) shaved
  Parmesan

1 Preheat the oven to
moderately hot 200°C
(400°F/Gas 6). Place
the ham bone in a
baking dish and roast
for 30 minutes, or until
golden brown.

2 Cover the lentils with
cold water and soak for
10 minutes. Drain well.
3 Heat the oil and 40 g
of the butter in a large
saucepan. Add the
onion, garlic, carrot and
celery and cook over
low heat for 10 minutes,
or until softened. Season
with plenty of freshly
ground black pepper.
Stir in the lentils and
cook for 1 minute. Add
the tomato, stock, bay
leaf and the ham bone.
Bring to the boil, then
reduce the heat to low.
Cover and simmer for
about 1 hour, or until
the lentils are very soft
and the soup reaches a
thick consistency.
4 Remove the ham
bone from the soup and
allow to cool slightly.
Cut the meat from the
bone and shred.
Remove and discard the
bay leaf from the soup.
5 Place half the soup
in a blender and blend
until smooth. Return
to the saucepan along
with the shredded ham,
parsley, Parmesan and
the remaining butter,
and stir until warmed
through.
6 Divide the soup
among four serving
bowls and serve.

PROSCIUTTO AND
ROCKET SALAD
1 Grill the prosciutto
slices under a hot grill
for 1–2 minutes each

side, or until crispy.
Allow to cool slightly
then break into smaller
pieces. Place the rocket,
red onion and three-
quarters of the prosciutto
in a bowl.
2 Combine the lemon
juice and olive oil and
season to taste with
salt and freshly ground
black pepper. Pour
the dressing over the
salad and toss lightly.
Garnish with the shaved
Parmesan and the
remaining prosciutto.
Serve with the soup,
if desired.

Nutrition per serve: Fat 43.5 g;
Protein 41 g; Carbohydrate 39 g;
Dietary Fibre 13.5 g; Cholesterol
94.5 mg; 2925 kJ (700 Cal)

BEEF AND CHILLI BEAN SOUP

Prep time: 15 minutes
Cooking time: 30 minutes
Serves 4

1 tablespoon oil
1 red onion, finely chopped
2 cloves garlic, crushed
2¹/2 teaspoons chilli flakes
2¹/2 teaspoons ground cumin
2¹/2 tablespoons finely chopped fresh coriander root and stem
1¹/2 teaspoons ground coriander
500 g lean beef mince
1 tablespoon tomato paste
4 tomatoes, peeled, seeded and diced
420 g can red kidney beans, drained and rinsed
2 litres beef stock
3 tablespoons chopped fresh coriander leaves
1/3 cup (80 g) sour cream

1 Heat the oil in a large saucepan over medium heat. Cook the onion for 2–3 minutes, or until softened. Add the garlic, chilli flakes, cumin, fresh and ground coriander, and cook for 1 minute. Add the mince and cook for 3–4 minutes, or until cooked through—break up any lumps with a spoon.
2 Add the tomato paste, tomato, beans and stock and bring to the boil. Reduce the heat, simmer for 15–20 minutes, or until rich and reduced

slightly. Remove any scum on the surface. Stir in the chopped coriander. Serve with sour cream.

Nutrition per serve: Fat 23.5 g; Protein 40 g; Carbohydrate 20 g; Dietary Fibre 8.5 g; Cholesterol 90 mg; 1880 kJ (450 Cal)

ROAST DUCK WITH RICE NOODLES

Prep time: 30 minutes + 20 minutes soaking
Cooking time: 45 minutes
Serves 4–6

15 g dried shiitake mushrooms
40 g dried black fungus
1 kg Chinese roast duck
1 tablespoon vegetable oil
2 teaspoons sesame oil
1 clove garlic, crushed
1 tablespoon grated fresh ginger
115 g fresh baby corn, cut in half on the diagonal
2 spring onions, finely sliced
200 g snow peas, cut in half on the diagonal
400 g bok choy, trimmed and cut into 2 cm lengths
100 ml oyster sauce
1 long fresh red chilli, seeded and cut into thin strips
1 tablespoon chopped fresh coriander leaves
1 tablespoon torn fresh Thai basil
400 g fresh rice noodle sheets, cut into 2 cm strips

1 Soak the shiitake and black fungus in boiling

water for 20 minutes, or until soft. Drain. Discard the stems from the shiitake and thinly slice the caps. Cut the fungus into bite-size pieces.
2 Remove the meat from the duck and thinly slice. Place the bones in a large saucepan with 2.75 litres water. Bring to the boil over high heat, then reduce the heat and simmer for 30 minutes. Remove any scum on the surface, then strain through a fine sieve.
3 Heat a wok over high heat, add the oils and swirl to coat. Add the garlic and ginger and fry for 30 seconds. Add the duck meat and stir-fry for 1 minute. Add the shiitake, black fungus, corn, spring onion, snow peas and bok choy and stir-fry for 2 minutes. Stir in the oyster sauce, chilli and 1.25 litres stock and simmer for 2 minutes, or until heated through. Stir in the herbs.
4 Cover the noodles with boiling water and soak for 1–2 minutes, or until tender. Separate gently and drain. Divide among the bowls, then ladle the soup on top.

Nutrition per serve (6): Fat 13 g; Protein 25 g; Carbohydrate 40 g; Dietary Fibre 3.5 g; Cholesterol 93.5 mg; 1565 kJ (375 Cal)

Beef and chilli bean soup (top), and Roast duck with rice noodles

PEA AND HAM SOUP

Prep time: 20 minutes
Cooking time:
    3 hours 10 minutes
Serves 4–6

2 tablespoons olive oil
2 onions, finely chopped
2 carrots, diced
2 celery sticks, diced
1 small turnip, finely
    chopped
2 cups (440 g) split green
    peas, rinsed and drained
1 smoked ham hock (800 g)
    (have your butcher cut it
    into smaller pieces)
2 bay leaves
2 sprigs fresh thyme
1/2 teaspoon ground ginger
1 tablespoon red wine
    vinegar

1 Heat the oil in a large saucepan over low heat. Add the onion, carrot, celery and turnip and cook for 5–6 minutes, or until softened. Add the split peas, ham hock, bay leaves, thyme, ground ginger and 2.5 litres water. Season. Slowly bring to the boil over medium heat, removing any scum that rises to the surface.
2 Reduce the heat and simmer, covered, for 2 hours 30 minutes to 3 hours, or until the peas are very soft and the ham falls off the bone.

Pea and ham soup (top), and Chicken laksa

Remove the ham bones and meat, cutting off any meat still attached to the bone, then cut the meat into smaller pieces. Return to the soup, discarding the bones. Remove the bay leaves and thyme. Stir the vinegar into the soup, season to taste and serve.

Nutrition per serve (6): Fat 11 g; Protein 29 g; Carbohydrate 35 g; Dietary Fibre 8.5 g; Cholesterol 34.5 mg; 1470 kJ (350 Cal)

CHICKEN LAKSA

Prep time: 30 minutes +
    10 minutes soaking
Cooking time: 20 minutes
Serves 4

Chicken balls
500 g chicken mince
1 small fresh red chilli,
    finely chopped
2 cloves garlic, finely
    chopped
1/2 small red onion,
    finely chopped
1 stem lemon grass
    (white part only),
    finely chopped
2 tablespoons chopped
    fresh coriander leaves

200 g dried rice vermicelli
1 tablespoon peanut oil
1/4 cup (75 g) good-quality
    laksa paste
1 litre chicken stock
2 cups (500 ml) coconut milk
8 fried tofu puffs, cut in half
    on the diagonal

90 g bean sprouts
2 tablespoons shredded
    fresh Vietnamese mint
3 tablespoons shredded
    fresh coriander leaves
lime wedges, to serve
fish sauce, to serve (optional)

1 To make the balls, process all the ingredients in a food processor until just combined. Roll tablespoons of mixture into balls with wet hands.
2 Place the vermicelli in a heatproof bowl, cover with boiling water and soak for 6–7 minutes. Drain well.
3 Heat the oil in a large saucepan over medium heat. Add the laksa paste and cook for 1–2 minutes, or until aromatic. Add the stock, reduce the heat and simmer for 10 minutes. Add the coconut milk and the balls and simmer for 5 minutes, or until the balls are cooked through.
4 Divide the vermicelli, tofu puffs and bean sprouts among four serving bowls and ladle the soup over the top, dividing the balls evenly. Garnish with the mint and coriander leaves. Serve with the lime wedges and, if desired, fish sauce.

Nutrition per serve: Fat 44.5 g; Protein 34 g; Carbohydrate 41 g; Dietary Fibre 4.5 g; Cholesterol 113 mg; 2900 kJ (690 Cal)

ZARZUELA

Prep time: 40 minutes
Cooking time:
    1 hour 15 minutes
Serves 4

1 cup (250 ml) dry white
    wine
1 large pinch saffron threads
3 tablespoons olive oil
500 g skinless firm white
    fish fillets (swordfish,
    monkfish or gemfish),
    cut into 2 cm cubes
500 g small calamari
    tubes, cleaned and
    cut into rings
1 onion, finely chopped
3 cloves garlic, thinly sliced
1 red capsicum, thinly sliced
1 green capsicum, thinly
    sliced
2 teaspoons paprika
400 g can diced tomatoes
20 g blanched almonds,
    finely chopped
1 bay leaf
1 small fresh red chilli
1 sprig fresh flat-leaf parsley
1/4 cup (60 ml) brandy or
    cognac
2 tablespoons lemon juice
1.5 litres fish stock
12 mussels, scrubbed and
    beards removed
12 clams, scrubbed
12 raw medium prawns,
    peeled, deveined and
    tails intact

Romesco sauce
3 tomatoes (about 450 g),
    halved and seeded
1 red capsicum, cut into
    four flat pieces
4 cloves garlic, unpeeled
20 blanched almonds,
    toasted
pinch cayenne pepper
2 tablespoons red wine
    vinegar
100 ml olive oil
1 tablespoon chopped
    fresh flat-leaf parsley

1 Place the wine and
saffron in a small bowl
and leave to infuse.
2 Meanwhile, heat half
the oil in a large saucepan
over medium–high heat.
Fry the fish in batches
for 2–3 minutes, or until
opaque and almost
cooked. Remove. Add
the calamari and cook
for 1 minute. Remove.
3 Add the remaining oil
to the pan and cook the
onion and garlic over
low heat for 5–6 minutes,
or until softened. Stir in
the capsicum slices and
paprika and cook for
1 minute. Stir in the
tomato, almonds and
infused wine. Season and
cook for 2–3 minutes.
4 Tie the bay leaf,
chilli and parsley sprig
together to form a
bouquet garni. Add to
the pan with the brandy,
lemon juice and stock,
then bring to the boil.
Reduce the heat and
simmer for 20 minutes.
Add the mussels and
clams, increase the
heat to high and cook,
covered, for 4–6 minutes,
or until the mussels open.
Discard any mussels that
don't open.

5 Return the fish and
calamari to the pan and
add the prawns. Reduce
the heat and simmer
for 5–6 minutes, or until
the prawns are cooked.
Discard the bouquet
garni and season.

ROMESCO SAUCE
1 Place the tomato and
capsicum skin-side-up
on a baking tray with the
garlic, then place under a
hot grill for 6 minutes,
or until the garlic
softens. Remove the
garlic. Grill the tomato
and capsicum for a
further 10 minutes, or
until the tomato skins
blister, then remove
the tomato. Grill the
capsicum for a further
5 minutes, or until the
skin blackens and blisters.
Place the capsicum in
a plastic bag to cool.
Remove the skin from
the garlic cloves, tomato
and capsicum.
2 Process the tomato,
garlic, capsicum, almonds
and cayenne pepper in
a food processor until
smooth. With the motor
running, slowly pour
in the vinegar, then
the oil. Add the parsley
and season to taste.
3 Stir 2–3 tablespoons of
the sauce through the
soup, and serve the
remainder with the soup.

Nutrition per serve: Fat 45.5 g;
Protein 74 g; Carbohydrate 16 g;
Dietary Fibre 6 g; Cholesterol
407 mg; 3545 kJ (845 Cal)

WINTER LAMB SHANK SOUP

Prep time: 30 minutes
Cooking time:
   3 hours 50 minutes
Serves 4

1 tablespoon olive oil
1.25 kg lamb shanks
2 onions, chopped
4 cloves garlic, chopped
1 cup (250 ml) red wine
2 bay leaves
1 tablespoon chopped fresh
   rosemary
2.5 litres beef stock
425 g can crushed tomatoes
3/4 cup (165 g) pearl barley,
   rinsed and drained
1 large carrot, diced
1 potato, diced
1 turnip, diced
1 parsnip, diced
2 tablespoons redcurrant
   jelly (optional)

1 Heat the oil in a large saucepan over high heat. Cook the shanks for 2–3 minutes, or until brown. Remove.
2 Add the onion to the pan and cook over low heat for 8 minutes, or until soft. Add the garlic and cook for 30 seconds, then add the wine and simmer for 5 minutes.
3 Add the shanks, bay leaves, half the rosemary and 1.5 litres of the stock to the pan. Season. Bring

Winter lamb shank soup (top), and French onion soup with goat's cheese croutes

to the boil over high heat. Reduce the heat and simmer, covered for 2 hours, or until the meat falls off the bone. Remove the shanks and cool slightly.
4 Take the meat off the bone and roughly chop. Add to the broth with the tomato, barley, the remaining rosemary and stock and simmer for 30 minutes. Add the vegetables and cook for 1 hour, or until the barley is tender. Remove the bay leaves, then stir in the redcurrant jelly.

Nutrition per serve: Fat 15.5 g; Protein 44 g; Carbohydrate 39 g; Dietary Fibre 8.5 g; Cholesterol 102.5 mg; 2155 kJ (515 Cal)

FRENCH ONION SOUP WITH GOAT'S CHEESE CROUTES

Prep time: 20 minutes
Cooking time: 1 hour
Serves 4

115 g butter
1.25 kg red onions, thinly
   sliced
2 large cloves garlic, crushed
3 1/2 tablespoons plain flour
1 1/4 cups (315 ml) dry white
   wine
1 litre beef stock
1 litre chicken stock
1 bay leaf
2 sprigs fresh thyme
1 1/2 tablespoons dry
   sherry

Goat's cheese croutes
1 sourdough bread stick, cut
   diagonally into 12 slices
2 tablespoons extra virgin
   olive oil
1 clove garlic, peeled
150 g goat's cheese, cut into
   12 slices
2 teaspoons fresh thyme

1 Melt the butter in a saucepan over low heat. Add the onion and cook, stirring occasionally, for 25 minutes, or until golden and it begins to caramelise. Stir in the garlic and flour and cook for 1 minute. Stir in the wine, then the stocks. Increase the heat to high, bring to the boil and cook for 1 minute. Add the bay leaf and thyme. Season. Reduce the heat to low and simmer, covered, for 30 minutes.
2 Remove the herbs from the soup and stir in the sherry. Serve with the croutes, if desired.

GOAT'S CHEESE CROUTES
1 Place the bread slices on a baking tray. Brush the tops with half the oil and grill for 1–2 minutes, or until golden. Rub with the garlic and top with a slice of cheese. Sprinkle with thyme and drizzle with the leftover oil. Season. (If desired, brown under a hot grill.)

Nutrition per serve: Fat 38.5 g; Protein 21 g; Carbohydrate 51 g; Dietary Fibre 7.5 g; Cholesterol 86 mg; 2885 kJ (690 Cal)

ROSEMARY AND WHITE BEAN SOUP WITH CRISPY KIPFLER WEDGES

Prep time: 15 minutes + overnight soaking
Cooking time:
  1 hour 5 minutes
Serves 4

3 cups (600 g) dried white cannellini beans
10 cloves garlic, unpeeled
1/3 cup (80 ml) extra virgin olive oil, plus extra for drizzling
3 large onions, sliced
3 cloves garlic, crushed
1 large sprig fresh rosemary (about 10 cm in length)
2.5 litres chicken stock
1 bay leaf

Crispy wedges
1 kg Kipfler potatoes, scrubbed and washed thoroughly
1/4 cup (60 ml) olive oil
2 teaspoons chopped fresh rosemary
1 teaspoon sea salt

1 Place the dried beans in a large bowl, cover with cold water and soak overnight. Drain and rinse.
2 Heat 3 tablespoons of the extra virgin olive oil in a large saucepan. Add the onion and cook over low heat, stirring occasionally, for 10 minutes, or until softened—do not allow it to brown. Add the garlic and continue to cook for 30 seconds. Add the cannellini beans, sprig of rosemary, chicken stock and the bay leaf. Increase the heat to high and bring to the boil. Reduce the heat to low, cover and simmer for 40–50 minutes, or until the beans are tender.
3 Meanwhile, preheat the oven to moderately hot 200°C (400°F/Gas 6). Toss the garlic cloves in 1 tablespoon of the olive oil, place on a baking tray and bake for 20–25 minutes, or until softened and golden. Remove the skins from the garlic cloves (the garlic should be soft) and set aside.
4 Remove the rosemary sprig and the bay leaf from the soup. Cool the soup slightly, then blend half in a blender with all the roasted garlic until smooth. Return to the saucepan and stir over medium heat until warmed through. Season with salt and freshly ground black pepper.
5 To serve, divide the soup evenly among four warmed serving bowls and drizzle the top with extra virgin olive oil.

CRISPY WEDGES
1 Preheat the oven to moderately hot 200°C (400°F/Gas 6). Bring a large saucepan of water to the boil, add the potatoes and boil for 5 minutes to partially cook through. Drain and cool slightly.
2 Cut the potatoes in half lengthways (or in quarters if too big). Place in a large bowl with the oil, garlic and chopped rosemary and toss together until well combined. Transfer to a baking dish and bake, turning halfway through, for 30–40 minutes, or until crisp and golden.
3 Season the crispy wedges with sea salt and serve with the soup.

Nutrition per serve: Fat 29 g; Protein 40 g; Carbohydrate 92 g; Dietary Fibre 31.5 g; Cholesterol 0 mg; 3230 kJ (770 Cal)

CHICKEN AND SPINACH RISONI SOUP

Prep time: 15 minutes
Cooking time: 35 minutes
Serves 4

1 tablespoon olive oil
1 leek, quartered lengthways and thinly sliced
2 cloves garlic, crushed
1 teaspoon ground cumin
1.5 litres chicken stock
2 chicken breast fillets (about 500 g)
1 cup (205 g) risoni
150 g baby English spinach leaves, roughly chopped
1 tablespoon chopped fresh dill
2 teaspoons lemon juice

1 Heat the oil in a large saucepan over low heat. Add the leek and cook for 8–10 minutes, or until soft. Add the garlic and cumin and cook for 1 minute. Pour the stock into the pan, increase the heat to high and bring to the boil. Reduce the heat to low, add the chicken fillets and simmer, covered, for 8 minutes. Remove the chicken from the broth, allow to cool slightly, then shred.
2 Stir the risoni into the broth and simmer for 12 minutes, or until *al dente*.
3 Return the chicken to the broth along with the spinach and dill. Simmer for 2 minutes, or until the spinach has wilted. Stir in the lemon juice, season to taste with salt and freshly ground black pepper and serve.

Nutrition per serve: Fat 13.5 g; Protein 38 g; Carbohydrate 39 g; Dietary Fibre 3.5 g; Cholesterol 82.5 mg; 1815 kJ (435 Cal)

GRILLED ITALIAN SAUSAGE AND VEGETABLE SOUP

Prep time: 20 minutes
Cooking time: 2 hours
Serves 4

500 g Italian pork sausages
200 g piece speck
1 tablespoon olive oil
1 large onion, chopped
3 cloves garlic, crushed
1 celery stick, cut in half and sliced
1 large carrot, cut into 1 cm cubes
1 bouquet garni (1 sprig parsley, 1 sprig oregano, 2 bay leaves)
1 small fresh red chilli, halved lengthways
400 g can diced tomatoes
1.75 litres chicken stock
300 g Brussels sprouts, cut in half from top to base
300 g green beans, cut into 3 cm lengths
300 g shelled broad beans, fresh or frozen
2 tablespoons chopped fresh flat-leaf parsley

1 Grill the sausages under a hot grill for 8–10 minutes, turning occasionally, or until brown. Remove and cut into 3 cm lengths. Trim and reserve the fat from the speck, then dice the speck itself.
2 Heat the oil in a large saucepan over medium heat. Add the speck and reserved speck fat and cook for 2–3 minutes, or until golden. Add the onion, garlic, celery and carrot, reduce the heat to low and cook for 6–8 minutes, or until softened. Discard the remains of the speck fat.
3 Stir in the sausages, bouquet garni, chilli and tomato and cook for 5 minutes. Add the stock, bring to the boil then reduce the heat and simmer for 1 hour. Add the Brussels sprouts, green beans and broad beans and simmer for a further 30 minutes. Discard the bouquet garni, then stir in the parsley. Season to taste. Divide among four bowls and serve.

Nutrition per serve: Fat 35.5 g; Protein 41 g; Carbohydrate 23 g; Dietary Fibre 12.5 g; Cholesterol 108.5 mg; 2375 kJ (570 Cal)

Chicken and spinach risoni soup (top), and Grilled Italian sausage and vegetable soup

LEMON-SCENTED SEAFOOD AND FENNEL BROTH WITH SKORDALIA CROUTES

Prep time: 20 minutes
Cooking time: 1 hour
Serves 4

11/2 large fennel bulbs, outer leaves removed (600 g) and fronds reserved
20 raw medium prawns, peeled, deveined and shells reserved
2.25 litres fish stock
1 large onion, chopped
4 cloves garlic, chopped
2 carrots, chopped
3 celery sticks, sliced
2 leeks, sliced
2 bay leaves
1 strip lemon rind (2 cm x 6 cm), white pith removed
2 sprigs fresh dill
5 fresh flat-leaf parsley stalks
3 sprigs fresh lemon thyme
11/2 cups (375 ml) dry white wine
450 g skinless firm white fish fillets (perch, snapper), cut into 2 cm cubes
2 tablespoons lemon juice
lemon wedges, to garnish

Skordalia croutes
1/2 French stick, cut into twelve 1 cm slices
250 g floury potatoes, cut into 2 cm cubes (desiree or King Edward)
3 large cloves garlic, crushed
pinch ground white pepper
1/3 cup (80 ml) olive oil
1 tablespoon lemon juice

1 Cut the stalk from the fennel and reserve. Cut the bulb in half lengthways, remove the core, and thinly slice the halves. Preheat the oven to moderately hot 200°C (400°F/Gas 6).

2 Place the prawn shells in a large saucepan and cover with 1 litre cold water. Bring to the boil over high heat and cook for 2 minutes. Drain, then discard the liquid. Wash the shells under cold running water to remove the scum, then return to the cleaned pan. Add the fish stock, reserved fennel stalk, onion, garlic, carrot, celery, leek, bay leaves, lemon rind, dill, parsley, thyme, white wine and 2 cups (500 ml) water and bring to the boil over high heat. Reduce the heat and simmer for 30 minutes.

3 Strain the broth through a fine sieve into a clean saucepan. Bring to a simmer over medium–low heat, add the fennel slices and simmer for 15 minutes. Add the prawns and fish and simmer for 3–5 minutes, or until the prawns change colour and the fish is cooked through. Season with salt and freshly ground black pepper and stir in the lemon juice to taste.

4 To serve, divide the soup among four serving bowls and garnish with the reserved fennel fronds and lemon wedges.

SKORDALIA CROUTES

1 Place the bread slices on a baking tray and bake for 8–10 minutes, or until golden, turning over halfway through.

2 Cook the potato in a saucepan of boiling water for 10 minutes, or until very soft. Drain, then mash with a potato masher or fork until very smooth. Stir in the garlic, white pepper and 1/2 teaspoon salt. Gradually mix in the oil until well combined. Stir in the lemon juice and keep warm. Spread the croutes with the skordalia. Serve with the soup, if desired.

Nutrition per serve: Fat 23 g; Protein 53 g; Carbohydrate 44 g; Dietary Fibre 4.5 g; Cholesterol 182.5 mg; 2770 kJ (660 Cal)

VIETNAMESE BEEF SOUP

Prep time: 15 minutes +
40 minutes freezing
Cooking time: 30 minutes
Serves 4

400 g rump steak, trimmed
1/2 onion
11/2 tablespoons fish sauce
1 star anise
1 cinnamon stick
pinch ground white pepper
1.5 litres beef stock
300 g fresh thin rice noodles
3 spring onions, thinly sliced
30 fresh Vietnamese mint
    leaves
90 g bean sprouts
1 small white onion, cut in
    half and thinly sliced
1 small fresh red chilli, thinly
    sliced on the diagonal
lemon wedges, to serve

1 Wrap the rump steak in plastic wrap and freeze for 40 minutes.
2 Meanwhile, place the onion, fish sauce, star anise, cinnamon stick, pepper, stock and 2 cups (500 ml) water in a large saucepan. Bring to the boil, then reduce the heat, cover and simmer for 20 minutes. Discard the onion, star anise and cinnamon stick.
3 Cover the noodles with boiling water and gently separate. Drain and refresh under cold water. Thinly slice the meat across the grain.
4 Divide the noodles and spring onion among four deep bowls. Top with the beef, mint, bean sprouts, onion and chilli. Ladle the hot broth over the top and serve with the lemon wedges.

Nutrition per serve: Fat 6 g;
Protein 32 g; Carbohydrate 37 g;
Dietary Fibre 2.5 g; Cholesterol
64 mg; 1390 kJ (330 Cal)

SEAFOOD CHOWDER

Prep time: 15 minutes
Cooking time: 1 hour
Serves 4–6

60 g butter
4 rashers bacon
    (about 250 g), diced
2 onions, finely chopped
2 leeks, thinly sliced
3 large cloves garlic, crushed
2 tablespoons plain flour
1.125 litres fish stock
1 bay leaf
3 sprigs fresh thyme
3 large potatoes, cut into
    1 cm cubes
500 g skinless firm white
    fish fillets (swordfish or
    gemfish), cut in 2 cm cubes
20 scallops, without roe
    (about 350 g)
290 g can baby clams,
    undrained
2 tablespoons chopped
    fresh flat-leaf parsley
13/4 cups (440 ml) thick
    cream

1 Melt 30 g of the butter in a large saucepan. Add the bacon and cook over medium heat for 2–3 minutes, or until golden. Reduce the heat to low and melt the remaining butter. Add the onion and leek and cook for 10 minutes, or until softened. Add the garlic and cook for 30 seconds, then add the flour and cook, stirring, for another 30 seconds.
2 Gradually stir the stock into the flour mixture until smooth and combined, then add the bay leaf and thyme and bring to the boil. Add the potato and simmer over low heat for 25–30 minutes, or until the potato has started to break down. Discard the bay leaf and thyme sprigs.
3 Add the fish, scallops, baby clams and their liquid, and return to a simmer for 4–5 minutes, or until the seafood is cooked. Stir in the parsley and cream, and season to taste. Continue to simmer over low heat for 2 minutes, or until the chowder is hot. Divide among serving bowls and serve.

Nutrition per serve (6): Fat 45.5 g;
Protein 45 g; Carbohydrate 20 g;
Dietary Fibre 3 g; Cholesterol
228.5 mg; 2775 kJ (665 Cal)

Vietnamese beef soup (top), and Seafood chowder

MINESTRONE WITH PESTO CROSTINI

Prep time: 30 minutes + overnight soaking
Cooking time: 2 hours
Serves 6–8

1 cup (200 g) dried cannellini beans
3 tablespoons olive oil
1 large onion, finely chopped
3 cloves garlic, crushed
3 tablespoons chopped fresh flat-leaf parsley
80 g piece pancetta, diced
1 carrot, diced
1 celery stick, cut in half lengthways and sliced
400 g can diced tomatoes
2.5 litres chicken or vegetable stock
2 potatoes, cut into 1 cm cubes
2 zucchini, halved lengthways and cut into 1 cm slices
100 g green beans, cut into 4 cm lengths
100 g English spinach leaves, shredded
8 fresh basil leaves, torn
100 g ditalini or other small pasta

Pesto crostini
1/2 French stick, cut into eight 1 cm slices on the diagonal
1/3 cup (50 g) pine nuts, toasted
1 cup (50 g) small fresh basil leaves
2 cloves garlic, crushed
1/2 cup (125 ml) olive oil
1/2 teaspoon sea salt

60 g pecorino cheese, finely grated

1 Place the dried beans in a large bowl, cover with cold water and soak overnight. Drain and rinse under cold water.
2 Heat the oil in a large saucepan. Add the onion, garlic, parsley and pancetta and cook over low heat for 10 minutes, or until the onion is soft and golden. Add the carrot and celery and cook for 5 minutes. Stir in the cannellini beans, tomato and stock and season with black pepper. Bring to the boil, reduce the heat and simmer, covered, stirring occasionally, for 1 hour 20 minutes.
3 Add the potato to the soup and simmer for 10 minutes, then add the zucchini, green beans, spinach, basil and the pasta, and simmer for 8–10 minutes, or until the vegetables and pasta are tender. Season to taste with salt and freshly ground black pepper.
4 To serve, divide the minestrone among the serving bowls.

PESTO CROSTINI
1 Preheat the oven to moderate 180°C (350°F/Gas 4). Place the bread slices on a baking tray and bake for 10 minutes, or until golden, turning over halfway through. Place the pine nuts, basil, garlic, oil and sea salt in a food processor and process until smooth. Transfer to a bowl and stir in the pecorino. Spread a little pesto on each crostini.
2 Serve the crostini with the minestrone. Any remaining pesto can be served at the table to be added to the soup, if desired.

Nutrition per serve (8): Fat 31 g; Protein 20 g; Carbohydrate 38 g; Dietary Fibre 9.5 g; Cholesterol 12.5 mg; 2095 kJ (500 Cal)

Note: You can use a 400 g can drained cannellini or borlotti beans instead of the dried beans, if preferred.

MOROCCAN LAMB, CHICKPEA AND CORIANDER SOUP

Prep time: 15 minutes +
  overnight soaking
Cooking time:
  2 hours 15 minutes
Serves 4–6

3/4 cup (165 g) dried
  chickpeas
1 tablespoon olive oil
850 g boned lamb leg,
  cut into 1 cm cubes
1 onion, chopped
2 cloves garlic, crushed
1/2 teaspoon ground
  cinnamon
1/2 teaspoon ground
  turmeric
1/2 teaspoon ground ginger
4 tablespoons chopped
  fresh coriander leaves
2 x 400 g cans diced
  tomatoes
1 litre chicken stock
2/3 cup (160 g) dried red
  lentils, rinsed
fresh coriander leaves,
  to garnish

1 Soak the chickpeas in cold water overnight. Drain, and rinse well.
2 Heat the oil in a large saucepan over high heat and brown the lamb in batches for 2–3 minutes. Reduce the heat to medium, return the lamb to the pan with the onion and garlic and cook for 5 minutes. Add the spices, season and cook for 2 minutes. Add the coriander, tomato, stock and 2 cups (500 ml) water and bring to the boil over high heat.
3 Add the lentils and chickpeas and simmer, covered, over low heat for 1 hour 30 minutes. Uncover and cook for 30 minutes, or until the lamb is tender and the soup is thick. Season. Garnish with coriander.

Nutrition per serve (6): Fat 9.5 g;
Protein 29 g; Carbohydrate 22 g;
Dietary Fibre 7.5 g; Cholesterol
51 mg; 1200 kJ (285 Cal)

ASPARAGUS SOUP WITH PARMESAN CRISPS

Prep time: 15 minutes
Cooking time: 30 minutes
Serves 4

720 g fresh asparagus,
  trimmed
1 tablespoon vegetable oil
30 g butter
1 large red onion, finely
  chopped
1 large leek, thinly sliced
2 large potatoes, cut into
  1 cm cubes
1.25 litres chicken stock
1/3 cup (80 ml) cream
1/3 cup (90 g) sour cream
1 tablespoon snipped fresh
  chives
60 g grated Parmesan

1 Roughly chop 630 g of the asparagus, then cut the rest into 6 cm pieces. Heat the oil and butter in a large saucepan over medium heat and cook the onion and leek for 5 minutes, or until soft. Add the potato, chopped asparagus and stock and bring to the boil over high heat. Reduce the heat and simmer for 8 minutes, or until the vegetables are tender. Blanch the remaining asparagus in a saucepan of boiling water.
2 Cool the soup, then purée. Return to the pan, stir in the cream for 1–2 minutes, or until heated through. Season. Garnish with sour cream, blanched asparagus and chives and serve.

PARMESAN CRISPS
1 Preheat the oven to moderately hot 190°C (375°F/Gas 5). Line three baking trays with baking paper and place four 9 cm egg rings on each tray. Sprinkle 5 g of the Parmesan into each ring in a thin layer—for a lacy edge, remove the rings. Bake for 5 minutes, or until melted and just golden brown. Cool.

Nutrition per serve: Fat 33.5 g;
Protein 17 g; Carbohydrate 19 g;
Dietary Fibre 5 g; Cholesterol
86 mg; 1840 kJ (440 Cal)

Moroccan lamb, chickpea and coriander soup (top), and Asparagus soup with Parmesan crisps

ROAST CAPSICUM SOUP WITH CARAMELISED ONION MUFFINS

Prep time: 30 minutes +
   10 minutes cooling
Cooking time:
   1 hour 20 minutes
Serves 4 (Makes 12 muffins)

4 red capsicums
   (about 1.5 kg), cut into
   quarters, seeds and
   membrane removed
2 tablespoons virgin olive oil
2 onions, roughly chopped
6 cloves garlic, crushed
1 litre chicken or vegetable
   stock
400 g can diced tomatoes
1 teaspoon chopped fresh
   thyme

Caramelised onion muffins
50 g butter
3 onions, thinly sliced
1 tablespoon soft brown
   sugar
2 cups (250 g) self-raising
   flour
3 tablespoons chopped
   fresh basil
3/4 cup (90 g) grated
   Cheddar
1 egg, lightly beaten
1 tablespoon olive oil
11/4 cups (315 ml) milk

1 Grill the capsicum skin-side-up under a hot grill in two batches for 10–12 minutes, or until blackened and blistered. Place in a plastic bag for 10 minutes to cool. Peel away the skin and cut the flesh into rough even-sized pieces.

2 Heat the oil in a large saucepan. Add the onion and garlic and cook over low heat for 10 minutes, or until soft but not browned. Add the stock, capsicum, tomato and thyme. Bring to the boil, then reduce the heat and simmer, covered, for 45 minutes. Cool slightly.

3 Blend the soup in batches in a blender until smooth.

4 To serve, divide the soup evenly among four serving bowls. Serve with the warm muffins, if desired.

CARAMELISED ONION MUFFINS

1 Preheat the oven to moderately hot 190°C (375°F/Gas 5). Lightly grease twelve 1/2 cup (125 ml) muffin holes. Melt the butter in a frying pan over low heat. Add the onion and cook, stirring, for 20 minutes, or until very soft. Add the sugar and cook, stirring, for 2 minutes. Cool.

2 Sift the flour into a large bowl, stir in the basil and cheese and season to taste with salt and freshly ground black pepper, then make a well in the centre.

3 Combine the egg, oil and milk and pour into the well all at once with three-quarters of the onion. Fold gently until just combined—the batter should still be lumpy. Spoon the mixture into the prepared muffin holes and top each with the remaining onion. Bake for 20–25 minutes, or until risen and golden.

Nutrition per serve: Fat 37.5 g; Protein 26 g; Carbohydrate 76 g; Dietary Fibre 4 g; Cholesterol 114 mg; 3105 kJ (740 Cal)

Note: This soup may also be served cold.

Storage: Muffins are best eaten on the day of baking but can be frozen, sealed in airtight freezer bags, for up to 3 months.

SPICY TOMATO SOUP WITH CHORIZO

Prep time: 15 minutes
Cooking time: 55 minutes
Serves 4–6

500 g chorizo sausage
2 tablespoons olive oil
3 onions, halved and sliced
3 cloves garlic, thinly sliced
1/2 teaspoon ground cumin
1 teaspoon paprika
1–2 small fresh red chillies, seeded and finely chopped
1.5 litres chicken stock
2 x 400 g cans diced tomatoes
4 tablespoons chopped fresh flat-leaf parsley

1 Fill a large, deep frying pan with 2–3 cm cold water. Add the chorizo, then bring to the boil over high heat. Reduce the heat and simmer, turning occasionally, for 15 minutes, or until the water evaporates, then continue to cook in any fat left in the pan for 3–4 minutes, or until lightly browned. Cool slightly and break into bite-size pieces.
2 Heat the oil in a large saucepan over medium heat, and cook the onion and garlic for 5–6 minutes, or until soft. Stir in the spices, chilli, chicken stock, tomato and half the parsley. Bring to the boil, add the chorizo, then reduce the heat and simmer for 20 minutes. Stir in the remaining parsley and serve.

Nutrition per serve (6): Fat 38 g; Protein 25 g; Carbohydrate 11 g; Dietary Fibre 3 g, Cholesterol 73.5 mg; 2045 kJ (490 Cal)

CHICKEN AND VEGETABLE SOUP

Prep time: 25 minutes + overnight refrigeration
Cooking time: 3 hours
Serves 6–8

Stock
2 tablespoons vegetable oil
1 large chicken (about 2 kg), quartered
2 large onions, chopped
2 large carrots, chopped
1 celery stick, chopped
1 sprig fresh flat-leaf parsley
1 sprig fresh thyme
2 bay leaves

1 large leek, thinly sliced
1 large potato, cut into 2 cm cubes
2 carrots, diced
150 g shelled peas
200 g green beans, trimmed and cut into 2 cm lengths
100 g yellow beans, trimmed and cut into 2 cm lengths
3 tablespoons chopped fresh flat-leaf parsley
cayenne pepper, to garnish

1 Heat the oil in a large stockpot and brown the chicken pieces over medium–high heat for 10 minutes. Remove the chicken. Add the onion, carrot and celery and cook, stirring, for 6–8 minutes, or until golden brown. Return the chicken to the pan with the herbs, 3 litres water and 1/2 teaspoon salt. Bring to the boil, reduce the heat and simmer, covered, for 2 hours, skimming the scum off the surface.
2 Remove the chicken pieces and cool the stock. Pour through a sieve into a large bowl. Discard the vegetables and herbs. Cover. Take the flesh off the chicken (discard the fat and bones) and shred into pieces. Cover. Refrigerate the stock and chicken overnight. Remove the layer of fat from the top of the stock.
3 Bring the stock to the boil in a saucepan. Add the leek, potato and carrot and simmer for 30 minutes, or until tender. Add the chicken, peas and beans and simmer for 15 minutes, or until the vegetables are tender. Stir in the parsley. Season with salt and cayenne pepper.

Nutrition per serve (8): Fat 6 g; Protein 20.5 g; Carbohydrate 8 g; Dietary Fibre 3 g; Cholesterol 57 mg; 700 kJ (165 Cal)

Spicy tomato soup with chorizo (top), and Chicken and vegetable soup

PRAWN GUMBO

Prep time: 15 minutes
Cooking time: 1 hour
Serves 4

2 tablespoons olive oil
1 large onion, finely chopped
3 cloves garlic, crushed
1 red capsicum, chopped
4 rashers bacon, chopped
1 1/2 teaspoons dried thyme
2 teaspoons dried oregano
1 teaspoon paprika
1/2 teaspoon cayenne
    pepper
1/4 cup (60 ml) sherry
1 litre fish stock
1/2 cup (100 g) long-grain rice
2 bay leaves
400 g can diced tomatoes
150 g okra, thinly sliced
850 g raw medium prawns,
    peeled and deveined
3 tablespoons finely chopped
    fresh flat-leaf parsley

1 Heat the oil in a large saucepan over low heat. Cook the onion, garlic, capsicum and bacon for 5 minutes, or until soft. Stir in the herbs and spices. Season. Add the sherry and cook until evaporated, then add the stock and 2 cups (500 ml) water. Bring to the boil. Add the rice and bay leaves, reduce the heat and simmer, covered, for 20 minutes.
2 Add the tomato and okra. Simmer, covered, for 20–25 minutes. Stir in the prawns and parsley, and simmer for 5 minutes,
or until the prawns are cooked through.

Nutrition per serve: Fat 15 g;
Protein 61 g; Carbohydrate 31 g;
Dietary Fibre 5 g; Cholesterol
341.5 mg; 2175 kJ (520 Cal)

CHICKPEA SOUP WITH SPICED PITTA BREAD

Prep time: 30 minutes
Cooking time:
    1 hour 15 minutes
Serves 4–6

1 tablespoon olive oil
1 large onion, chopped
5 cloves garlic, chopped
1 large carrot, chopped
1 bay leaf
2 celery sticks, chopped
1 teaspoon ground cumin
1/2 teaspoon ground
    cinnamon
3 x 425 g cans chickpeas,
    drained and rinsed
1.25 litres chicken stock
1 tablespoon finely chopped
    fresh flat-leaf parsley, plus
    extra to garnish
1 tablespoon finely chopped
    fresh coriander leaves
2 tablespoons lemon juice
extra virgin olive oil, to drizzle

Spiced pitta bread
40 g butter
2 tablespoons olive oil
2 cloves garlic, crushed
1/8 teaspoon, plus a pinch,
    ground cumin
1/8 teaspoon, plus a pinch,
    ground cinnamon
1/8 teaspoon, plus a pinch,
    cayenne pepper
1/2 teaspoon sea salt
4 small pitta breads, split

1 Heat the oil in a large saucepan. Cook the onion over medium heat for 3–4 minutes, or until soft. Add the garlic, carrot, bay leaf and celery and cook for 4 minutes, or until they start to caramelise.
2 Stir in the spices and cook for 1 minute. Add the chickpeas, stock and 1 litre water and bring to the boil. Reduce the heat and simmer for 1 hour. Allow to cool.
3 Remove the bay leaf and purée the soup. Return to the cleaned pan and stir over medium heat until warmed. Stir in the herbs and lemon juice. Season.
4 Drizzle with oil and garnish with parsley.

SPICED PITTA BREAD
1 Melt the butter and oil in a saucepan over medium heat. Add the garlic, spices and salt and cook for 1 minute. Place the pitta (smooth-side-up) on a lined tray, and grill for 1–2 minutes, or until golden. Turn and brush with the spiced butter. Grill until golden.

Nutrition per serve (6): Fat 18.5 g;
Protein 15 g; Carbohydrate 41 g;
Dietary Fibre 9.5 g; Cholesterol
16 mg; 1620 kJ (385 Cal)

Prawn gumbo (top),
and Chickpea soup with
spiced pitta bread

ZUCCHINI SOUP WITH BACON AND ONION BREAD

Prep time: 20 minutes
Cooking time: 1 hour
Serves 4

60 g butter
2 large leeks (white part only), thinly sliced
4 cloves garlic, crushed
1.25 kg zucchini, coarsely grated
1.75 litres chicken stock
1/3 cup (80 ml) cream

Bacon and onion bread
1 tablespoon olive oil
2 large onions, sliced
200 g bacon rashers, chopped into 1 cm pieces
3 cups (375 g) plain flour
1/2 teaspoon bicarbonate of soda
1 teaspoon baking powder
3 eggs, lightly beaten
1 cup (250 ml) milk
1 egg yolk
1 tablespoon milk, extra

1 Melt the butter in a saucepan over medium heat. Cook the leek, stirring once or twice, for 2–3 minutes, or until it starts to soften. Reduce the heat to low, add the garlic and cook, covered, stirring once or twice, for 10 minutes, or until the leek is really soft—do not allow it to brown. Add the zucchini and cook, uncovered, for 4–5 minutes. Pour in the chicken stock and bring to the boil over high heat. Reduce the heat to medium–low and simmer for 20 minutes, or until soft.

2 Let the soup cool slightly and blend half in a blender until smooth. Return to the pan, stir in the cream and gently reheat over medium heat until warmed through. Season to taste with salt and freshly ground black pepper.

3 Serve the soup with slices of the bacon and onion bread, if desired.

BACON AND ONION BREAD

1 Preheat the oven to moderate 180°C (350°F/Gas 4). Lightly grease a 24 cm x 12 cm loaf tin and line the base with baking paper.

2 Heat the oil in a large frying pan over medium heat, add the onion and cook for 5 minutes, or until soft and starting to brown. Add the bacon and cook for a further 10 minutes, or until the bacon is crisp and brown. Drain on crumpled paper towels, then allow to cool completely.

3 Sift the plain flour, bicarbonate of soda, baking powder and 1/4 teaspoon salt into a large bowl and make a well in the centre. Add the egg and milk and stir until just combined.

Turn out onto a lightly floured work surface and top with the bacon and onion mixture, kneading it evenly into the dough (be careful not to overwork the dough). Gently press the dough into the prepared tin and lightly brush the top with the combined egg yolk and extra milk. Bake for 30–40 minutes, or until golden brown.

Nutrition per serve: Fat 42 g; Protein 35 g; Carbohydrate 95 g; Dietary Fibre 12 g; Cholesterol 148 mg; 3745 kJ (895 Cal)

SOUTH AMERICAN BLACK BEAN SOUP

Prep time: 15 minutes +
    overnight soaking
Cooking time:
    1 hour 10 minutes
Serves 4

1 1/2 cups (330 g) black turtle
    beans (black kidney beans)
1 tablespoon vegetable oil
1 onion, finely chopped
1 leek, finely chopped
2 cloves garlic, crushed
2 teaspoons ground cumin
4 rashers bacon, diced
1 litre chicken stock
1/3 cup (90 g) sour cream
1 1/2 tablespoons snipped
    fresh chives

1 Soak the black beans in a bowl of cold water overnight. Drain.
2 Heat the oil in a large saucepan over medium heat and cook the onion, leek, garlic and cumin for 2–3 minutes, or until soft. Add the bacon and cook for a further 2–3 minutes, or until lightly browned.
3 Add the black beans, stock and 2 cups (500 ml) water to the pan and bring to the boil over high heat. Reduce the heat and simmer for 1 hour, or until the black beans are tender. Season to taste with salt and freshly ground black pepper.
4 Cool slightly and blend half the soup in batches in a blender until smooth. Return to the saucepan and stir through the unblended soup. Spoon into bowls, dollop with sour cream and garnish with the snipped chives.

Nutrition per serve: Fat 26 g; Protein 32 g; Carbohydrate 38 g; Dietary Fibre 16.5 g; Cholesterol 56.5 mg; 2070 kJ (495 Cal)

CAULIFLOWER AND ALMOND SOUP WITH HOT CHEESE ROLLS

Prep time: 20 minutes
Cooking time: 30 minutes
Serves 4

75 g blanched almonds
1 tablespoon olive oil
1 large leek (white part only),
    chopped
2 cloves garlic, crushed
1 kg cauliflower, cut into
    small florets
2 desiree potatoes
    (about 370 g), cut into
    1.5 cm pieces
1.75 litres chicken stock

Cheese rolls
4 round bread rolls
40 g softened butter
120 g Cheddar, grated
50 g Parmesan, grated

1 Preheat the oven to moderate 180°C (350°F/Gas 4). Place the almonds on a baking tray and toast for 5 minutes, or until golden.
2 Heat the oil in a large saucepan over medium heat and cook the leek for 2–3 minutes, or until softened. Add the garlic and cook for 30 seconds, then add the cauliflower, potato and stock. Bring to the boil, then reduce the heat and simmer for 15–20 minutes, or until the vegetables are very tender. Allow to cool for 5 minutes.
3 Blend the soup with the almonds in batches in a blender until smooth. Season to taste with salt and pepper. Return to the cleaned pan and stir over medium heat until heated through, if needed. Serve with the cheese rolls, if desired.

CHEESE ROLLS
1 Split the rolls and butter both sides. Combine the grated cheeses and divide evenly among the rolls. Sandwich together and wrap in foil. Bake in the oven for 15–20 minutes, or until the cheese has melted.

Nutrition per serve: Fat 43 g; Protein 35 g; Carbohydrate 49 g; Dietary Fibre 10.5 g; Cholesterol 67.5 mg; 3015 kJ (720 Cal)

South American black bean soup (top), and Cauliflower and almond soup with hot cheese rolls

BEEF BROTH WITH MUSHROOMS AND INDIVIDUAL BREAD AND BUTTER PUDDINGS

Prep time: 20 minutes +
    overnight refrigeration
Cooking time:
    4 hours 30 minutes
Serves 4

Stock
1 kg beef bones
1 kg beef osso buco
2 large onions, chopped
2 large carrots, chopped
3 celery sticks, chopped
2 large leeks, chopped
1 cup (250 ml) red wine
2 teaspoons tomato paste
8 sprigs fresh flat-leaf parsley
1 bay leaf
6 sprigs fresh thyme
10 black peppercorns

40 g butter
400 g button mushrooms,
    thinly sliced
2 cloves garlic, crushed
1/3 cup (80 ml) medium-dry
    sherry
2 tablespoons finely
    chopped fresh flat-leaf
    parsley

Bread and butter puddings
20 g butter, softened
2 cloves garlic, crushed
4 slices white bread,
    crusts removed
2 eggs, lightly beaten
1 cup (250 ml) light cream

1 Preheat the oven to hot 220°C (425°F/Gas 7). Place the beef bones and osso buco in two large roasting tins, then scatter with the onion, carrot, celery and leek. Roast for 1 hour, turning halfway through cooking. Transfer the bones and vegetables to a large stockpot or saucepan and add 3.5 litres cold water.
2 Drain the fat from the roasting tins. Add 1/2 cup (125 ml) of the wine to each tin and stir over high heat, scraping up any sediment stuck to the bottom. Transfer to the stockpot with the tomato paste, herbs and peppercorns. Bring to the boil over high heat, removing any scum that rises to the surface. Reduce the heat to low and simmer for 3 hours, continuing to remove the scum on the surface.
3 Remove the osso buco bones from the stock and allow to cool. Discard all the remaining bones. Remove the meat from the osso buco bones and shred. Cover and refrigerate.
4 Strain the stock into a large bowl and cool completely. Cover and refrigerate overnight. Remove the layer of fat from the surface.
5 Melt the butter in a large saucepan and cook the mushrooms over low heat for 10 minutes, or until they start to brown. Add the garlic and cook for 30 seconds. Add the sherry, increase the heat to medium–high and cook for 5 minutes, or until reduced. Pour in 1 litre of the stock and 1 litre water and bring to the boil over high heat. Reduce the heat and simmer for 10 minutes. Stir in the shredded meat until warmed through and sprinkle with the parsley. Keep warm.

BREAD AND BUTTER PUDDINGS
1 Preheat the oven to moderately hot 200°C (400°F/Gas 6). Lightly grease a twelve hole mini muffin tin. Combine the butter and garlic and spread on both sides of the bread. Cut each slice into three strips, then cut the strips into three again—you should have nine squares per slice (36 in total).
2 Combine the egg and cream and season. Dip the squares of bread into the egg mixture and allow to soak for a few minutes. Place 3 squares into each muffin hole and pour on any leftover egg mixture. Bake for 10–15 minutes, or until puffed and golden.
3 Serve the soup with the puddings, if desired.

Nutrition per serve: Fat 38 g; Protein 39 g; Carbohydrate 17 g; Dietary Fibre 4 g; Cholesterol 247 mg; 2445 kJ (585 Cal)

TOMATO AND CAPSICUM SOUP WITH POLENTA AND OLIVE STICKS

Prep time: 40 minutes +
    30 minutes refrigeration
Cooking time: 1 hour
Serves 4–6

2 tablespoons vegetable oil
2 tablespoons olive oil
2 red onions, finely chopped
2 cloves garlic, crushed
1 tablespoon ground cumin
1/4 teaspoon ground
    cayenne pepper
2 teaspoons paprika
2 red capsicums, diced
1/3 cup (90 g) tomato paste
1 cup (250 ml) dry white wine
2 x 400 g cans chopped
    tomatoes
2 long fresh red chillies,
    seeded and chopped
2 cups (500 ml) chicken or
    vegetable stock
3 tablespoons chopped
    fresh flat-leaf parsley
4 tablespoons chopped
    fresh coriander leaves

Polenta and olive sticks
2 cups (500 ml) chicken or
    vegetable stock
1 1/4 cups (185 g) coarse
    polenta
100 g pitted Kalamata olives,
    chopped
1/2 cup (125 ml) olive oil,
    to deep-fry

1 Heat the oils in a large saucepan over medium heat and cook the onion and garlic for 2–3 minutes, or until soft. Reduce the heat to low, add the spices and cook for 1–2 minutes. Add the capsicum and cook for 5 minutes. Stir in the tomato paste and wine, simmering for 2 minutes, or until reduced slightly. Add the tomato, chilli, stock and 2 cups (500 ml) water. Season. Simmer for 20 minutes. Purée the soup with the herbs.

POLENTA AND OLIVE STICKS

1 Grease a 19.5 x 30 cm lamington tray. Bring the stock and 2 cups (500 ml) water to the boil in a saucepan. Slowly add the polenta in a fine stream, whisking until smooth. Reduce the heat to low. Cook, stirring constantly, for 15–20 minutes, or until it starts to come away from the side. Stir in the olives, then spoon into the tray, smoothing the surface. Cover and chill for 30 minutes, or until firm. Cut into 6.5 x 1.5 cm sticks.
2 Heat the oil in a large deep frying pan to 190°C (375°F), or until a cube of bread browns in 10 seconds. Cook the sticks in batches on each side for 1–2 minutes, or until crisp. Drain well, and serve with the soup.

Nutrition per serve (6): Fat 29.5 g; Protein 8 g; Carbohydrate 35 g; Dietary Fibre 5 g; Cholesterol 0 mg; 1915 kJ (455 Cal)

PEA, LETTUCE AND BACON SOUP

Prep time: 20 minutes
Cooking time: 10 minutes
Serves 4

2 tablespoons vegetable oil
2 onions, finely chopped
200 g bacon rashers,
    chopped
1 kg frozen baby peas,
    thawed
1.5 litres chicken stock
1.2 kg iceberg lettuce,
    finely shredded
watercress sprigs, to garnish

1 Heat the oil in a large saucepan over medium heat. Add the onion and bacon and cook for 2–3 minutes, or until soft, but not browned. Add the peas, stock and half the lettuce to the pan, then simmer for 5 minutes, or until the peas are tender. Season.
2 Allow the soup to cool slightly, then blend until smooth. Return to the pan with the remaining lettuce and stir over medium–low heat until warmed through. Serve, garnished with the watercress.

Nutrition per serve: Fat 22 g; Protein 31 g; Carbohydrate 31 g; Dietary Fibre 20 g; Cholesterol 29.5 mg; 1855 kJ (445 Cal)

Tomato and capsicum soup with polenta and olive sticks (top), and Pea, lettuce and bacon soup

PUMPKIN AND CARROT SOUP WITH HERB SCONES AND HORSERADISH CREAM

Prep time: 20 minutes
Cooking time: 40 minutes
Serves 4–6

40 g butter
1 large onion, chopped
2 cloves garlic, crushed
500 g carrots, sliced
1/2 cup (125 ml) orange juice
750 g butternut pumpkin, peeled and roughly chopped
1.5 litres chicken stock
1 tablespoon snipped fresh chives

Herb scones
3 cups (375 g) plain flour
1 1/2 tablespoons baking powder
50 g butter, softened
1/2 cup (60 g) grated Cheddar
1 tablespoon finely chopped fresh flat-leaf parsley
1 tablespoon finely chopped fresh basil
1 tablespoon finely chopped fresh dill
1 tablespoon finely chopped fresh chives
1 1/4 cups (315 ml) milk

Horseradish cream
1 1/2 tablespoons horseradish cream
1 cup (250 g) light sour cream

1 Melt the butter in a large saucepan over medium heat and cook the onion for 5 minutes, or until soft and starting to brown. Add the garlic and carrot and cook for another 5 minutes, or until starting to soften. Pour in the orange juice and bring to the boil over high heat. Add the pumpkin, stock and 2 cups (500 ml) water and return to the boil. Reduce the heat and simmer for 30 minutes, or until the carrot and pumpkin are soft.

2 Blend the soup in batches in a blender until smooth—add a little more stock if you prefer a thinner consistency.

3 Return to the cleaned pan and reheat. Season to taste with salt and freshly ground black pepper. Divide the soup among serving bowls and garnish with the chives.

HERB SCONES

1 Preheat the oven to hot 220°C (425°F/Gas 7). Lightly grease a 30 cm x 30 cm baking tray. Sift the flour, baking powder and 1/4 teaspoon salt into a large bowl. Rub in the butter, using your fingertips until the mixture resembles fine breadcrumbs. Make a well in the centre of the mixture and add the cheese, parsley, basil, dill, chives and almost all the milk. Mix lightly with a flat-bladed knife, to a soft dough—add some more milk if needed.

2 Press the scone dough into a 28 cm x 12 cm rectangle. Cut in half lengthways, then cut into six widthways to give 12 pieces in total. Gently shape each piece into a neat square using lightly-floured hands. Place on the prepared tray leaving a 2 cm space between each scone. Brush the tops with a little milk and bake for 10 minutes, or until golden. Keep warm.

HORSERADISH CREAM

1 Combine the horseradish cream, sour cream, salt and freshly ground black pepper in a small bowl until smooth.

2 To serve, cut the scones in half, top with some of the horseradish cream mixture, then serve with the soup, if desired.

Nutrition per serve (6): Fat 29 g; Protein 20 g; Carbohydrate 60 g; Dietary Fibre 7 g; Cholesterol 84 mg; 2565 kJ (610 Cal)

AVGOLEMONO WITH CHICKEN

Prep time: 25 minutes
Cooking time: 35 minutes
Serves 4

1 carrot, chopped
1 large leek, chopped
2 bay leaves
2 chicken breast fillets
2 litres chicken stock
1/3 cup (80 g) short-grain rice
3 eggs, separated
1/3 cup (80 ml) lemon juice
2 tablespoons chopped
   fresh flat-leaf parsley
40 g butter, chopped

1 Place the carrot, leek, bay leaves, chicken and stock in a large saucepan. Bring to the boil over high heat, then reduce the heat and simmer for 10–15 minutes, or until the chicken is cooked. Strain into a clean pan and reserve the chicken.
2 Add the rice to the liquid, bring to the boil, then reduce the heat and simmer for 15 minutes, or until tender. Cut the chicken into 1 cm cubes.
3 Whisk the egg whites in a clean dry bowl until stiff peaks form. Beat in the yolks until light and creamy, whisk in the lemon juice, then 1 cup (250 ml) of the soup. Remove the soup from the heat and gradually whisk in the egg mixture. Add the chicken and stir over low heat for 2 minutes— do not boil or the egg will scramble. Serve at once with a sprinkle of parsley and dot of butter.

Nutrition per serve: Fat 21.5 g; Protein 40 g; Carbohydrate 22 g; Dietary Fibre 1.5 g; Cholesterol 260 mg; 1840 kJ (440 Cal)

Note: This soup will not stand well—make just before serving.

GOULASH SOUP WITH DUMPLINGS

Prep time: 30 minutes
Cooking time: 2 hours
Serves 4–6

3 tablespoons olive oil
1 kg chuck or round steak,
   cut into 1 cm cubes
2 large onions, chopped
3 cloves garlic, crushed
1 green capsicum, chopped
1 1/2 teaspoons caraway
   seeds, ground
3 tablespoons sweet
   paprika
1/4 teaspoon ground
   nutmeg
pinch cayenne pepper
1/2 teaspoon sea salt
400 g can diced tomatoes
2 litres chicken stock
350 g potatoes, cut into
   2 cm cubes
1 green capsicum, julienned
2 tablespoons sour cream

Dumplings
1 egg
3 tablespoons finely grated
   Parmesan
75 g self-raising flour
pinch cayenne pepper

1 Heat half the oil in a saucepan, and brown the beef in batches for 1–2 minutes. Remove. Heat the remaining oil in the same pan over low heat. Add the onion, garlic and chopped capsicum and cook for 5–6 minutes, or until softened. Stir in the spices and salt for 1 minute.
2 Return the beef to the pan and stir to coat. Stir in the tomato and stock and bring to the boil. Reduce the heat to low and simmer, covered, for 1 hour 15 minutes. Add the potato and cook for 30 minutes. Stir in the julienned capsicum and sour cream. Season.
3 To make the dumplings, mix together all the ingredients and a pinch of salt with a fork to form a soft dough (add 1–2 tablespoons water if necessary). Turn onto a lightly floured surface and knead for 5 minutes, or until smooth. Roll 1/2 teaspoonfuls of the dough into balls, drop into the simmering soup and cook for 6 minutes, or until cooked. Serve.

Nutrition per serve (6): Fat 21 g; Protein 47 g; Carbohydrate 27 g; Dietary Fibre 4.5 g; Cholesterol 140.5 mg; 2030 kJ (485 Cal)

Avgolemono with chicken (top), and Goulash soup with dumplings

CHICKEN MULLIGATAWNY WITH WHOLEMEAL PURIS

Prep time: 40 minutes +
 overnight refrigeration +
 30 minutes standing
Cooking time:
 4 hours 15 minutes
Serves 6 (Makes 12 puris)

Stock
1.5 kg chicken
1 carrot, chopped
2 celery sticks, chopped
4 spring onions, cut into
 3 cm lengths
2 cm piece fresh ginger,
 sliced

20 g ghee
1 large onion, finely
 chopped
3 cloves garlic, crushed
8 curry leaves
3 tablespoons madras
 curry paste
1 cup (250 g) red lentils,
 washed and drained
2 tomatoes, peeled and
 chopped
1/3 cup (80 g) short-grain
 rice
1 cup (250 ml) coconut
 cream
2 tablespoons fresh
 coriander leaves,
 chopped
mango chutney, to serve

Puris
1 cup (150 g) plain
 wholemeal flour
1 cup (125 g) plain flour
10 g ghee
vegetable oil, to deep-fry

1 To make the stock, place all the ingredients and 4 litres cold water in a large stockpot or saucepan. Bring to the boil, removing any scum that rises to the surface. Reduce the heat to low and simmer, partly covered, for 3 hours. Continue to remove any scum from the surface.
2 Carefully remove the chicken and cool. Strain the stock into a bowl and cool. Cover and refrigerate overnight. Discard the skin and bones from the chicken and shred the flesh into small pieces. Cover and refrigerate overnight.
3 To make the soup, remove the fat from the surface of the stock. Melt the ghee in a large saucepan over medium heat. Cook the onion for 5 minutes, or until soft. Add the garlic and curry leaves and cook for 1 minute. Add the curry paste, cook for 1 minute, then stir in the lentils until coated. Pour in the stock and bring to the boil over high heat, removing any scum on the surface. Reduce the heat, add the tomato and simmer for 30 minutes, or until the lentils are completely soft.
4 Bring a large saucepan of water to the boil. Add the rice and cook for 12 minutes, stirring once or twice. Drain. Stir the rice into the soup with the chicken and coconut cream until warmed through—don't allow it to boil or it will curdle. Season. Sprinkle with the coriander and serve with the mango chutney.

PURIS
1 Sift the wholemeal and plain flours and 1/2 teaspoon salt in a large bowl. Rub the ghee into the flour and add 1/2 cup (125 ml) tepid water. Mix the dough with a knife, then turn out onto a lightly floured surface. Knead for 5 minutes, or until smooth. Cover and rest for 30 minutes.
2 Roll the dough on a lightly floured surface, to about 1 mm thick. Cut 12 circles with an 8 cm round cutter, rolling out each circle to smooth out the edges—ensure they're not much larger. Cover.
3 Fill a large deep-sided frying pan one-third full of oil and heat to 170°C (325°F), or until a cube of bread browns in 20 seconds. Cook 2 dough rounds at a time for 20 seconds. Lightly press in the centre with a slotted spoon, turn and cook for 20 seconds, or until puffed and golden. Drain. Repeat with the remaining dough.

Nutrition per serve: Fat 31.5 g;
Protein 37 g; Carbohydrate 62 g;
Dietary Fibre 11 g; Cholesterol
76 mg; 2830 kJ (675 Cal)

CORN AND CHEDDAR SOUP WITH HERB CORN MUFFINS

Prep time: 30 minutes
Cooking time: 50 minutes
Serves 6 (Makes 12 muffins)

5 large corn cobs (1.5 kg)
1 tablespoon olive oil
200 g bacon, cut into
    2 cm pieces
60 g butter
2 large onions, finely
    chopped
2 cloves garlic, crushed
3 tablespoons plain flour
1.5 litres chicken stock
2 large floury potatoes,
    cut into 2 cm cubes
250 g Cheddar, grated
3/4 cup (185 ml) cream
1/4 teaspoon cayenne
    pepper

Herb corn muffins
2 cups (250 g) plain flour
1 tablespoon baking powder
pinch cayenne pepper
1 egg, lightly beaten
50 g butter, melted
11/4 cups (315 ml) milk
3/4 cup (90 g) grated
    Cheddar
1 cup (180 g) drained
    canned corn kernels
1 tablespoon finely chopped
    fresh flat-leaf parsley
1 teaspoon fresh thyme
    leaves, finely chopped
2 teaspoons chopped
    fresh chives

1 Cut the kernels from each corn cob with a sharp knife, then cook in a large saucepan of boiling water for 3 minutes. Drain.
2 Heat the oil in a large saucepan over medium heat and cook the bacon for 5 minutes, or until brown and crisp. Drain on paper towel. Drain any oil from the pan.
3 Melt the butter in the pan over medium–low heat and cook the onion for 10 minutes, or until soft. Add the garlic and cook for 30 seconds. Stir in the flour and continue to cook for 2 minutes, or until the flour begins to foam. Gradually pour in the chicken stock, stirring, then add the potato and corn. Bring to the boil over high heat, then reduce the heat and simmer for 20–25 minutes, or until the potato is soft.
4 Stir the Cheddar through the soup until melted. Allow to cool slightly, then blend in a blender until smooth. Return to the cleaned saucepan and stir in the cream until warmed through. To serve, divide among serving bowls and garnish with cayenne pepper and the crispy bacon.

HERB CORN MUFFINS
1 Preheat the oven to moderately hot 200°C (400°F/Gas 6). Grease twelve 1/2 cup (125 ml) muffin holes.

2 Lightly sift the flour, baking powder, cayenne pepper and 1/4 teaspoon salt into a large bowl and make a well in the centre. Combine the egg, butter and milk in a jug, then pour into the dry ingredients all at once and gently mix until just combined.
3 Carefully stir in the cheese, corn, parsley, thyme and chives—take care not to overmix. Spoon the mixture into the prepared holes and bake for 15–20 minutes, or until puffed and golden. Transfer to a wire rack to cool slightly.
4 Serve the muffins with the soup, if desired.

Nutrition per serve: Fat 62.5 g;
Protein 41 g; Carbohydrate 77 g;
Dietary Fibre 11 g; Cholesterol
205.5 mg; 4295 kJ (1025 Cal)

RED LENTIL, BURGHUL AND MINT SOUP

Prep time: 20 minutes
Cooking time: 45 minutes
Serves 4–6

2 tablespoons olive oil
1 large red onion, finely chopped
2 cloves garlic, crushed
2 tablespoons tomato paste
2 tomatoes, finely chopped
2 teaspoons paprika
1 teaspoon cayenne pepper
2 cups (500 g) red lentils
1/4 cup (50 g) long-grain rice
2.125 litres chicken stock
1/4 cup (45 g) fine burghul (bulgar wheat)
2 tablespoons chopped fresh mint
2 tablespoons chopped fresh flat-leaf parsley
1/3 cup (90 g) plain Greek-style yoghurt
1/4 preserved lemon, pulp removed, rind washed and julienned

1 Heat the oil in a saucepan over medium heat. Add the onion and garlic and cook for 2–3 minutes, or until soft. Stir in the tomato paste, tomato and spices, and cook for 1 minute.
2 Add the lentils, rice and stock, then cover and bring to the boil over high heat. Reduce the heat and simmer for 30–35 minutes, or until the rice is cooked.
3 Stir in the burghul and herbs, then season to taste. Divide the soup among serving bowls, garnish with yoghurt and preserved lemon and serve immediately.

Nutrition per serve (6): Fat 10 g; Protein 22 g; Carbohydrate 40 g; Dietary Fibre 11 g; Cholesterol 4 mg; 1390 kJ (330 Cal)

Note: This soup will thicken on standing, so if reheating you may need to add more liquid.

CHICKEN, MUSHROOM AND MADEIRA SOUP

Prep time: 20 minutes + 20 minutes soaking
Cooking time: 1 hour 20 minutes
Serves 4

10 g porcini mushrooms
25 g butter
1 leek (white part only), thinly sliced
250 g pancetta or bacon, chopped
200 g Swiss brown mushrooms, roughly chopped
300 g large field mushrooms, roughly chopped
2 tablespoons plain flour
1/2 cup (125 ml) Madeira
1.3 litres chicken stock
1 tablespoon olive oil
2 chicken breast fillets (about 200 g each)
1/3 cup (80 g) light sour cream
2 teaspoons chopped fresh marjoram, plus whole leaves, to garnish

1 Soak the mushrooms in 1 cup (250 ml) boiling water for 20 minutes.
2 Melt the butter in a large saucepan over medium heat and cook the leek and pancetta for 5 minutes, or until the leek is softened. Add all the mushrooms and the porcini soaking liquid, and cook for a further 10 minutes.
3 Stir in the flour and cook for 1 minute. Add the Madeira and cook, stirring, for 10 minutes. Stir in the stock, bring to the boil, then reduce the heat and simmer for 45 minutes. Cool slightly.
4 Heat the oil in a frying pan and cook the chicken for 4–5 minutes each side, or until cooked through. Remove from the pan and thinly slice.
5 Blend the soup until smooth. Return to the cleaned saucepan, add the sour cream and marjoram and stir over medium heat for 1–2 minutes to warm through. Season. Top with the chicken and garnish with marjoram.

Nutrition per serve: Fat 28.5 g; Protein 44 g; Carbohydrate 15 g; Dietary Fibre 4.5 g; Cholesterol 130.5 mg; 2180 kJ (520 Cal)

Red lentil, burghul and mint soup (top), and Chicken, mushroom and Madeira soup

SPICY SEAFOOD AND ROASTED CORN SOUP WITH CHEESE AND CORIANDER QUESADILLAS

Prep time: 15 minutes
Cooking time:
  1 hour 20 minutes
Serves 4

2 corn cobs (700 g)
1 tablespoon olive oil
1 red onion, finely chopped
1 small fresh red chilli,
  finely chopped
1/2 teaspoon ground allspice
4 vine-ripened tomatoes,
  peeled and finely diced
1.5 litres fish stock or light
  chicken stock
300 g boneless firm white
  fish fillets (ling or perch),
  diced
200 g fresh crab meat
200 g peeled raw prawns,
  roughly chopped
1 tablespoon lime juice

Quesadillas
4 flour tortillas (19 cm)
2/3 cup (85 g) grated
  Cheddar
4 tablespoons fresh
  coriander leaves
2 tablespoons olive oil

1 Preheat the oven to moderately hot 200°C (400°F/Gas 6). Peel back the husks on the corn cobs (making sure they stay intact at the base) and remove the silks. Fold the husks back over the corn, place in a baking dish and bake in the oven for 1 hour, or until the corn is tender.

2 Meanwhile, heat the oil in a large saucepan over medium heat. Add the onion and cook for 5 minutes, or until soft. Add the chopped chilli and ground allspice and cook for 1 minute, then add the tomato and stock and bring to the boil. Reduce the heat and simmer, covered, for 45 minutes.

3 Remove the kernels from the corn cobs with a sharp knife, add to the soup and simmer, uncovered, for 15 minutes.

4 Add the fish, crab and prawn meat to the soup and gently simmer for 5 minutes, or until the seafood is cooked. Stir in the lime juice and serve.

QUESADILLAS

1 Top one tortilla with half the cheese and 2 tablespoons of the coriander. Season well with salt and ground black pepper, then top with another tortilla.

2 Heat 1 tablespoon of the oil in a large frying pan and cook the quesadilla for 30 seconds on each side, or until browned and the cheese just begins to melt. Repeat with the remaining tortillas, cheese, coriander and olive oil.

3 Cut each quesadilla into eight wedges and serve immediately with the soup.

Nutrition per serve: Fat 24 g; Protein 50 g; Carbohydrate 38 g; Dietary Fibre 7 g; Cholesterol 172.5 mg; 2370 kJ (565 Cal)

Notes: Tortillas are thin rounds of unleavened bread made from ground maize (cornmeal).

Fresh tortillas are eaten as bread, used as a plate and spoon, or filled to make other meals such as tacos and enchiladas—fillings include selections of shredded cooked meat, refried beans, fish, cheese, guacamole, shredded lettuce and salsa.

SPAGHETTI AND MEATBALL SOUP

Prep time: 25 minutes
Cooking time: 35 minutes
Serves 4

150 g spaghetti, broken
    into 8 cm lengths
1.5 litres beef stock
3 teaspoons tomato paste
400 g can diced tomatoes
3 tablespoons fresh basil
    leaves, torn
shaved Parmesan, to garnish

Meatballs
1 tablespoon oil
1 onion, finely chopped
2 cloves garlic, crushed
500 g lean beef mince
3 tablespoons finely chopped
    fresh flat-leaf parsley
3 tablespoons fresh
    breadcrumbs
2 tablespoons finely grated
    Parmesan
1 egg, lightly beaten

1 Cook the spaghetti in a large saucepan of boiling water according to packet instructions until *al dente*. Drain. Put the stock and 2 cups (500 ml) water in a large saucepan and slowly bring to a simmer.

2 To make the meatballs, heat the oil in a small frying pan over medium heat and cook the onion for 2–3 minutes, or until soft. Add the garlic and cook for 30 seconds. Allow to cool.

3 Combine the mince, parsley, breadcrumbs, Parmesan, egg, the onion mixture, and salt and pepper. Roll a heaped teaspoon of mixture into a ball, making 40 in total.

4 Stir the tomato paste and tomato into the stock and simmer for 2–3 minutes. Drop in the meatballs, return to a simmer and cook for 10 minutes, or until cooked through. Stir in the spaghetti and basil to warm through. Season. Garnish with Parmesan.

Nutrition per serve: Fat 17 g; Protein 39 g; Carbohydrate 36 g; Dietary Fibre 3.5 g; Cholesterol 117.5 mg; 1905 kJ (455 Cal)

PORK CONGEE

Prep time: 15 minutes
Cooking time:
    1 hour 45 minutes
Serves 4–6

1 1/2 cups (300 g) long-grain
    rice, thoroughly rinsed
1/2 star anise
2 spring onions (white part
    only)
4 cm x 4 cm piece fresh
    ginger, cut into slices
3.5 litres chicken stock
1 tablespoon peanut oil
2 cloves garlic, crushed
1 teaspoon grated fresh
    ginger, extra
400 g pork mince

ground white pepper
1/4 cup (60 ml) light soy
    sauce
sesame oil, to drizzle
6 fried dough sticks
    (see Note)

1 Place the rice in a large saucepan with the star anise, spring onions, sliced ginger and stock. Bring to the boil, reduce the heat and simmer for 1 hour 30 minutes, stirring occasionally.

2 Heat the oil in a frying pan over high heat. Cook the garlic and grated ginger for 30 seconds. Add the mince and cook for 5 minutes, or until browned, breaking up any lumps with the back of a spoon.

3 Discard the star anise, spring onions and ginger from the soup, add the mince mixture and simmer for 10 minutes. Season with white pepper and stir in the soy sauce. Serve with a drizzle of sesame oil and the dough sticks.

Nutrition per serve (6): Fat 10 g; Protein 24 g; Carbohydrate 46 g; Dietary Fibre 0.5 g; Cholesterol 40 mg; 1530 kJ (365 Cal)

Note: Fried dough sticks are available at Chinese bakeries and speciality shops and are best eaten soon after purchasing. If not, reheat in a moderately hot (200°C/400°F/Gas 6) oven for 5 minutes, then serve.

Spaghetti and meatball soup (top), and Pork congee

ROASTED EGGPLANT AND CHICKPEA SOUP WITH GARLIC AND PARSLEY SALSA

Prep time: 20 minutes
Cooking time:
   1 hour 15 minutes
Serves 4

90 ml olive oil
1 onion, finely chopped
2 cloves garlic, finely
   chopped
2 teaspoons ground
   cumin
1 teaspoon paprika
1/4 teaspoon ground
   ginger
1/4 teaspoon ground
   cinnamon
1/4 teaspoon ground
   allspice
1 tablespoon tomato
   paste
2 x 400 g cans diced
   tomatoes
1.125 litres chicken or
   vegetable stock
800 g eggplant, cut into
   1.5 cm cubes
425 g can chickpeas,
   drained and rinsed

Garlic and parsley salsa
1/2 cup (25 g) finely
   chopped fresh flat-leaf
   parsley
2 teaspoons finely chopped
   fresh oregano
2 cloves garlic, finely
   chopped
1/2 teaspoon ground cumin,
   dry roasted
11/2 tablespoons olive oil
pinch sea salt

1 Heat 1 tablespoon of the olive oil in a large saucepan over medium heat. Add the onion and cook for 5 minutes, or until soft. Add the garlic and cook for a further minute. Add the ground cumin, paprika, ginger, cinnamon and allspice and cook, stirring, for 30 seconds, or until fragrant. Stir in the tomato paste and cook for another 30 seconds. Add the canned tomato and the stock and bring to the boil over high heat. Reduce the heat, then simmer, covered, for 30 minutes.
2 Meanwhile, preheat the oven to moderately hot 200°C (400°F/ Gas 6). Place the eggplant and the remaining olive oil in a roasting tin and toss together until well coated. Bake, stirring once or twice, for 30 minutes, or until golden brown.
3 Add the drained chickpeas to the soup and simmer, uncovered, for a further 15 minutes. Stir in the cooked eggplant and simmer for another 15 minutes. Season to taste with salt and freshly ground black pepper.

GARLIC AND PARSLEY SALSA
1 Place the parsley, oregano, garlic, cumin, oil and salt in a bowl and stir until combined.
2 Divide the soup among four serving bowls and top with a spoonful of the salsa. Serve immediately.

Nutrition per serve: Fat 23.5 g; Protein 13 g; Carbohydrate 28 g; Dietary Fibre 12.5 g; Cholesterol 0 mg; 1555 kJ (370 Cal)

Note: One of the most versatile and popular legumes in many parts of the world, chickpeas were first grown in the Levant and ancient Egypt. There are two kinds of chickpea, the large white garbanzo and the smaller brown dessi. Some of the most popular Middle Eastern dishes, including hummus, have chickpeas as their basis. They can be boiled, roasted, ground, mashed and milled and are available dried and canned.

ORANGE SWEET POTATO SOUP WITH SPICY LAVASH STRIPS

Prep time: 30 minutes + 1 hour standing
Cooking time: 1 hour
Serves 4–6

40 g butter
2 onions, chopped
2 cloves garlic, crushed
1 kg orange sweet potato, peeled and chopped
1 large celery stick, chopped
1 large green apple, peeled, cored and chopped
1 1/2 teaspoons ground cumin
2 litres chicken stock
1/2 cup (125 g) plain Greek-style yoghurt

Spicy lavash strips
1 cup (125 g) plain flour
1/2 teaspoon sugar
3 tablespoons dried onion flakes
1/2 teaspoon chilli flakes
1/2 teaspoon ground cumin
20 g chilled butter, cut into small pieces
1/3 cup (80 ml) milk

1 Melt the butter in a large saucepan over low heat. Add the onion and cook, stirring occasionally, for 10 minutes, or until soft. Add the garlic, sweet potato, celery and apple and continue to cook for 5–7 minutes, or until well coated. Add the chicken stock and the remaining cumin and bring to the boil over high heat. Reduce the heat and simmer for 25–30 minutes, or until the sweet potato is very soft.

2 Cool the soup slightly and blend in batches until smooth. Return to the cleaned pan and gently stir over medium heat until warmed through. Season with salt and freshly ground black pepper. Divide among serving bowls and top each serve with a dollop of yoghurt. Serve with the spicy lavash strips, if desired.

SPICY LAVASH STRIPS
1 Sift the flour into a large bowl, stir in the sugar, onion flakes, chilli flakes, ground cumin and 1/2 teaspoon salt. Rub in the butter until the mixture resembles fine breadcrumbs. Add the milk and cut the liquid in with a flat-bladed knife to form a dough.
2 Turn onto a lightly floured surface and gather into a smooth ball. Knead for 1–2 minutes, or until smooth. Cover with a clean cloth and rest for 1 hour.
3 Preheat the oven to moderately hot 190°C (375°F/Gas 5). Divide the dough into three equal portions, rolling out each portion in a rectangular shape to 1 mm thick. Cut into 4 x 12 cm rectangular strips and place on a lined baking tray. Bake for 15–20 minutes, or until crisp and lightly golden.

Nutrition per serve (6): Fat 12.5 g; Protein 12 g; Carbohydrate 54 g; Dietary Fibre 6 g; Cholesterol 33 mg; 1560 kJ (375 Cal)

Note: To enhance the flavour of this dish, you can replace the ground cumin with the same quantity of dry-roasted cumin seeds. Simply dry-roast 2 teaspoons of cumin seeds in a small frying pan over medium heat for 30–60 seconds, or until fragrant. Grind to a fine powder in a spice grinder or mortar and pestle, then use the quantities as directed in the recipe.

Index